TAEKWONDO

NEIL MORRIS

Heinemann
LIBRARY

H **www.heinemann.co.uk**
Visit our website to find out more information about **Heinemann Library** books.
To order:
☎ Phone 44 (0) 1865 888066
▤ Send a fax to 44 (0) 1865 314091
💻 Visit the Heinemann Bookshop at www.heinemann.co.uk/library to browse our catalogue and order online.

First published in Great Britain by Heinemann Library, Halley Court, Jordan Hill, Oxford OX2 8EJ, a division of Reed Educational and Professional Publishing Ltd. Heinemann is a registered trademark of Reed Educational & Professional Publishing Limited.

OXFORD MELBOURNE AUCKLAND JOHANNESBURG BLANTYRE
GABORONE IBADAN PORTSMOUTH NH (USA) CHICAGO

Designed by Ken Vail Graphic Design, Cambridge
Illustrations by Simon Girling & Associates (Mike Lacey)
Originated by Dot Gradations
Printed by Wing King Tong in Hong Kong.

ISBN 0 431 11041 7
05 04 03 02 01
10 9 8 7 6 5 4 3 2 1

J796.8155
1365118

British Library Cataloguing in Publication Data

Morris, Neil, 1946–
Taekwondo. – (Get going! Martial arts)
1. Taekwondo
I. Title
796.8'153

Acknowledgements
The Publishers would like to thank the following for permission to reproduce photographs: Blitz, p. 9; Sylvio Dokov, p. 29; European Press Agency/P A News, pp. 4, 25; Fiona Hanson, p. 5; Mark Hupton, p. 6; Rex Features, p. 7. All other photographs by Trevor Clifford.

Cover photograph reproduced with permission of P A News.

Our thanks to Sandra Beale, Director of Coaching, National Association of Karate and Martial Art Schools, and to Kevin Hornsey, Chairman, National Executive Committee, British Taekwondo Control Board, for their comments in the preparation of this book.We would also like to thank Sam, Craig, Paul, Charlotte, Adrian, Taylor, Scott, Nathan, Andrew and Emma, of Keon Taekwondo Club, Northampton.

Every effort has been made to contact copyright holders of any material reproduced in this book. Any omissions will be rectified in subsequent printings if notice is given to the Publisher.

Words appearing in the text in bold, **like this**, are explained in the Glossary.

CONTENTS

 Do remember that martial arts need to be taught by a qualified, registered instructor, or teacher. Don't try any of the techniques and movements in this book without such an instructor present.

WHAT IS TAEKWONDO?

Taekwondo is a Korean martial art that is practised by 50 million people throughout the world. Its name means 'way of the foot and the fist', and taekwondo is best known for its use of spectacular flying kicks. It is sometimes called simply kick-boxing, but this is not a term that martial artists use. Taekwondo combines some of the movements of Japanese **karate** and Chinese **kung fu**.

Like other martial arts, taekwondo offers students the opportunity to practise demanding physical routines and learn about self-defence, as well as taking part in a competitive sport. It is based on strong mental discipline, and it teaches students to do things correctly, showing self-control and respect for others.

Top-level taekwondo competitors show how exciting the sport is.

AN OLYMPIC SPORT

At the Olympic Games held in Sydney, Australia, in 2000, taekwondo became the second martial art to be accepted as an Olympic sport. Judo was first seen at the Tokyo Olympics in 1964. In Sydney 52 men and 48 women competed for taekwondo gold medals.

The Olympic form of the sport follows the rules laid down by the World Taekwondo Federation. Competitors wear body protectors and headgear, and full-contact kicks and punches are made to specific target areas. By contrast, the form of the sport promoted by the International Taekwondo Federation allows only light contact.

WHERE TO LEARN AND PRACTISE

This book tells you how to set about starting taekwondo. It also shows and explains some taekwondo **techniques**, so that you can understand and practise them. But you must always remember that you cannot learn a martial art just from a book. To study and take up taekwondo seriously you must go to regular lessons with a qualified teacher, so that you learn all the techniques properly and then repeat and practise them many times.

Choose your club carefully. It should have an experienced teacher and it should belong to an approved national taekwondo association. The list on page 31 shows where you can get information and lists of clubs.

Taekwondo students in South Korea demonstrate their skills.

TAEKWONDO – THE BEGINNINGS

Taekwondo is an ancient martial art. The oldest records are about 2000 years old. They are from a period in Korean history known as the Three Kingdoms that began in 37 BC. In an ancient royal tomb in one of the kingdoms, called Koguryo, wall paintings show unarmed fighters practising **techniques** that are very similar to those of modern taekwondo.

In another of the kingdoms, called Silla, the young sons of nobles were taught to become strong warriors, and to be members of a group called the *hwarang* (flower of youth). A form of combat known as *taekkyon* was an important part of their training to become military leaders. It was seen as a way of building strength by using the hands and feet freely, and at the same time training the body to adapt to any danger or attack.

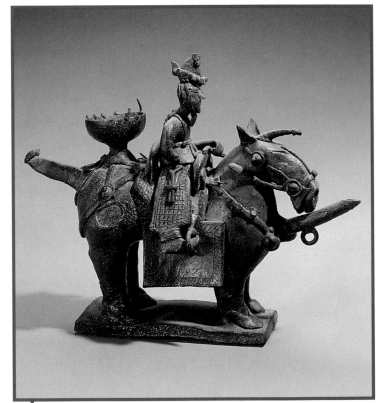

This stoneware model of a warrior on horseback was made in the ancient Korean kingdom of Silla.

This martial art was taught to go along with five principles for young warriors – to be loyal to their kingdom, obedient to their parents, trustworthy to their friends, never to retreat in battle, and to kill an enemy only when absolutely necessary.

FLYING KICKS

Travelling hwarang warriors spread the knowledge of their martial art, then known as *subak*. The flying kick techniques were probably developed to knock men off their horses. By the time of the Korean Yi dynasty (1392–1910), subak was taught more for health and fitness. Then, when the Japanese occupied Korea from 1910 to 1945, all Korean martial arts were banned.

In 1955, various Korean martial arts schools came together to agree on one style. Major-General Choi Hong Hi, a black belt martial artist, founded the agreed style. Two years later it was given the name taekwondo. Study of the art spread quickly in Korean schools and colleges.

Taekwondo students taking part in the opening ceremony of the Seoul Olympics in 1988. Twelve years later taekwondo became a full Olympic sport.

In 1973, the first world championships were held in Seoul, the capital of South Korea. Thirty countries took part in the tournament. Korea took first place, and representatives from all the countries founded the World Taekwondo Federation. Since then the world championships have been held in countries all over the world, including the United States and Canada.

EQUIPMENT

Taekwondo is practised and performed in a special white outfit called a *dobok*. It is best to buy a dobok through your club, but you don't need one immediately. For the first few sessions a tracksuit or T-shirt and training bottoms will probably do, but check this with the club first.

The dobok is all white, although versions approved by some taekwondo organizations have a black trim for more advanced students. It is made up of a pair of trousers and a loose jacket tied at the waist with a belt. Doboks are usually sold with a white belt, which is the right colour for a beginner. Make sure that your dobok is large enough so that your movements are not restricted in any way.

It is very important to treat your dobok with respect. It should always be clean, washed and ironed. A neat and tidy appearance shows that you have the right attitude to training. Inside the training hall or gymnasium, called a *dojang*, you must always have bare feet. A pair of flip-flops is useful to keep your feet clean as you walk from the changing room to the dojang.

PUTTING ON THE DOBOK

Put the trousers on first. Many dobok bottoms are elasticated at the waist. If they have a drawstring, pull it and tie it in a bow. Next put on the jacket. Some jackets have a v-neck instead of an open front and are slipped over the head.

Putting on the dobok top.

1 To tie the belt, pull it across your stomach first, keeping the two ends equal.

2 Wrap the belt round your waist twice, starting from the front.

3 Cross the left end over the right, then pull it up behind both layers of the belt.

4 Finally, tie the free ends together right over left and pull them through to finish the knot. Make sure the two ends are equal in length.

Doing up the belt.

 SAFETY

In order not to harm yourself or anyone else, do not wear a watch or any jewellery. Keep your fingernails and toenails trimmed short. Tie long hair back, but never with metal clips.

Make sure that you are fit enough to be very active, and do not train if you are ill. Exercise should not hurt, so never push yourself to the point where you feel pain. Tell your instructor if you suffer from any medical condition.

All martial arts can be dangerous if they are not performed properly. Never fool around inside or outside the training hall – or at home or in school – by showing off or pretending to have a real fight.

 PROTECTIVE EQUIPMENT

Headguards, mouthguards, chest protectors and groin guards should be worn when practising any form of competition or sparring. How much protection you wear will depend on the style your club follows.

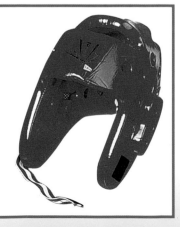

IN THE DOJANG

It is important for any martial arts student to show respect to everyone and everything to do with their sport, including the training hall. When they go into the dojang, taekwondo students bow to their instructor or to the senior grade. If there is no one in the dojang when you enter, stop inside the entrance and bow to the middle of the hall. Always do the same when you leave the hall. The taekwondo bow is called *kyungye* in Korean.

MAKING A BOW

The kyungye is made before and after every exercise, and to an opponent before and after each contest. Students also bow when they pass equipment such as safety pads to each other.

To perform the bow, first put your heels and toes together and place your hands against the side of your thighs. Then bow smoothly by bending your upper body forwards, but not too far. Dip your head so your eyes look downwards. Count to two as you hold that position. Then straighten up again.

There is a saying that 'taekwondo begins and ends with courtesy'.

This is how to sit when your instructor is talking to you.

THE RIGHT ATTITUDE

Courtesy is one of the five important principles that show that students have the right attitude towards taekwondo. When your instructor is talking to you in the dojang, you should sit in a cross-legged position and listen carefully and politely. Remember that during a training session students should never chatter, fool about or fidget.

The other principles are integrity, perseverance, self-control and indomitable spirit. 'Integrity' means being honest, always doing your very best and not pretending or cheating. 'Perseverance' involves keeping going and never giving up, even when things get difficult. Self-control is essential in all martial arts. You must never lose your temper or get too **aggressive** with a fellow student or an opponent. 'Indomitable spirit' means showing that you cannot be defeated by any difficulty.

WARMING UP

Taekwondo is hard, physical exercise. It is important to warm your body up and stretch your muscles before training, so that you do not injure yourself. Always start a session with some warm-up exercises. Begin by walking or jogging on the spot for a couple of minutes, before doing some stretching exercises.

STRETCHING EXERCISES

Try these exercises to stretch your muscles before starting to train.

WINDMILLS

You can turn your arms like the sails of a windmill.

1 Stand up straight with your arms by your sides.

2 Swing your left arm forwards, up and round behind you in a circle. Keep your arm straight and reach high at the top of the circle. Repeat five times.

3 Do the same exercise with the right arm.

4 Then repeat the exercise with both arms at the same time.

UPPER BACK STRETCH

1 Stand up straight and clasp your hands together behind your back, intertwining your fingers.

2 Lift your hands up as high as you can and as far away from your back as possible. Hold this position for a count of five and then return to the starting position.

3 Repeat the exercise five times.

GLUTEAL STRETCH

The gluteus is the buttocks, or bottom, made up of the largest muscles in the human body.

1 Stand up straight and raise your right knee. Intertwine your fingers under the knee and hold this position for a count of ten.

2 Repeat the exercise with the left leg.

3 Repeat the whole exercise three times.

❗ IMPORTANT

● Never exercise too hard when it is very hot or humid.

● Never exercise or practise taekwondo when you are ill or injured.

● Try not to breathe too hard and fast when you are exercising or resting.

● Don't hold your breath while you are exercising or practising.

● When you are stretching, you should always remain comfortable and your muscles should not hurt. If you feel pain, stop at once.

● Begin your taekwondo exercises immediately after warming up.

STANCES

As a taekwondo student you have many basic **techniques** to learn before you can start to put moves together. There are four different sets of basic techniques, made up of **stances**, **blocks**, punches and kicks.

In taekwondo, stances are not just a way of standing. They are fighting positions that need to be learned and practised. They form the beginning and the foundation of all the other techniques. Practising them also helps to build up the right muscles and develop good balance. When advanced students are **sparring**, or taekwondo competitors are actually fighting, the stances between moves are held for only a split second as the fighters flow from one technique to another.

READY STANCE

This first stance (called *choonbi* in Korean) is sometimes called the first or beginning position. When you stand in this way, it means you are ready to practise taekwondo.

1 Stand with your feet a shoulder-width apart and your weight spread evenly between them.

2 Bring your fists in front of your chest and then lower them to your waist. Your knuckles should be in a slight v-shape.

3 Keep looking straight ahead. This position is used at the start of all the **patterns** you will learn (see pages 22–23).

FORWARD STANCE

1 This stance *(apkoobi)* is a good launch-pad for front attacks and defences.

2 Step forward on your right foot, with the front leg slightly bent and the back leg straight. Draw both fists up to your sides at waist level, ready for the next movement.

BACK STANCE

1 This stance *(dwit koobi)* presents a small and difficult target to the opponent.

2 From the ready stance, step forward with your left foot, turning your body to the right and putting most of your weight on your back, right leg.

HORSERIDING STANCE

1 It is easy to see why this is called the horseriding stance *(choochoom soegi)*. It is a strong position for attacking and defending to either side.

2 Spread your legs so that your feet are two shoulder-widths apart, and bend your knees so that you are half-squatting. Keep your back straight.

3 Pull your fists back, at waist level.

BLOCKING

In martial arts and many other sports, players have to learn to defend themselves against attack. **Blocks** are especially important in taekwondo, as a form of self-defence to stop yourself from being hurt. In competition, they stop the opponent from scoring. Most blocks are made with the arms and hands, though some are performed with the legs and feet. Blocks can be learned without an opponent or partner, and form part of many taekwondo **patterns**.

DOWN BLOCK

The downward or low block *(arae makki)* is used against kicks and punches aimed at the lower body. It can be learned and practised in the forward **stance**.

1 With your right foot forward, cross your right fist over your chest to near your left ear.

2 To make the down block against an imaginary opponent's arm or leg, sweep your right arm down in a circular movement across your body, blocking with the forearm. At the same time, put your left fist into position at waist level.

RISING BLOCK

The rising or upper block *(eolgol makki)* is a good defence against straight punches to the face, and overhead attacks to the head. Like the down block, it is performed in the forward stance.

1 Put your right arm above your left shoulder and your left arm straight down towards your groin.

2 Sweep your left arm up, blocking with the outside of the forearm. At the same time, put your right fist into position at waist level.

INNER BLOCK

The inner or inside block *(momtong makki)* protects against straight attacks to the upper body.

1 With your left foot forward, raise both arms towards the left side of your head.

2 Then put your right fist in the usual position at waist level as you quickly move your left fist to deflect the blow.

KOREAN NUMBERS

In taekwondo, counting is often done in Korean:

One	*hana*	Six	*yasot*
Two	*dul*	Seven	*elgub*
Three	*set*	Eight	*yodol*
Four	*net*	Nine	*ahob*
Five	*dasot*	Ten	*yol*

STRIKING

In taekwondo, you can strike with your hands and arms in many different ways. One of the most important strikes is the straight punch. For this it is important to make a fist correctly, so that your punch is as powerful as possible but does not hurt you, the striker. Power comes from having the fist, wrist, elbow, shoulder and other parts of your body all acting together. You can practise punching against an opponent holding a pad.

MAKING A FIST

1 To make a fist, first fold your fingers down. Then fold your thumb across the index and middle fingers, to lock them in.

2 In a taekwondo punch you aim at the target with the first two knuckles. Keep your fist straight in line with your arm, so that the wrist does not bend when you hit the target. But make sure that your arm stays slightly bent when you punch, so as not to put too much strain on your elbow.

The correct way to make a fist.

! When making a fist, never put your thumb inside your fingers. If your thumb is on the inside it can be badly hurt, or even broken, when you punch.

KIHAP

The Korean term *kihap* is used to show that your mind and body are working together. During any powerful move, you must add all your energy and determination. It helps if at the same time you give a short, explosive shout. As well as helping to give power, calling out the kihap gives you confidence, clearing your mind of fear and scaring your opponent.

PRACTISING STRAIGHT PUNCHING

Start in the horseriding stance, both fists palm-upwards.

1 Push your right fist forward to punch an imaginary opponent. Just before you punch, turn your fist palm-downwards.

2 Pull your right fist back, and at the same time push your left fist forwards, so that your two fists pass each other in front of you.

3 Before your right arm reaches your body, turn it so that the palm is upwards. At the same time turn your left fist round into the punching position and make an imaginary punch. Remember to strike with your first two knuckles.

KNIFE-HAND AND PALM-HEEL

In taekwondo you can also strike with the outside edge of your hand (called knife-hand or chop), with the inside edge (called ridge-hand), with the heel of your hand, or with the elbow.

For the palm-heel strike, bend your wrist back, hold the thumb against the side of the hand, and keep your fingers curved and away from the palm.

KICKING

Taekwondo is famous for its spectacular kicks, which can be extremely powerful. They are particularly effective because legs are longer than arms, which means that kicks can reach further than punches. Most taekwondo kicks begin with the leg bent at the knee. The leg is then straightened to hit the target with different parts of the foot, but never the toes. It is important to keep the leg slightly bent, so as not to put too much strain on the knee.

You will probably learn to do front, round, side and back kicks before you attempt the amazing jumping and flying taekwondo kicks.

FRONT KICK

For this kick *(ap chagi)* start off in the ready **stance** and then slide your left foot forward. Bend your knees and keep your left fist up to guard your face.

1 Bring your right leg forward and raise your right foot, pulling the toes back.

2 When your right knee is high, thrust out your right leg, pushing your hips into the kick and keeping your toes pulled back. Imagine that you are hitting the target with the ball of your foot – the hard area just behind your toes. Keep your guard up during the kick.

BACK KICK

This kick *(dwi chagi)* involves turning your back on your opponent, so you should only use it as a surprise move or after another attacking **technique**.

Keep your eyes on your opponent as you lift your right foot and thrust it back in a straight line, heel first.

JUMPING FRONT KICK

Jumping kicks are made with both feet off the floor. To turn these into flying kicks, you have to take a few running steps, so that you move towards your opponent, and kick as you are in the air.

1 For the jumping front kick, first bring your left leg up high.

2 Then, as you snap that leg down again, lift your right knee and jump into the air.

3 Do a high front kick with your right leg.

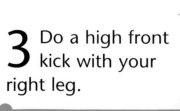

PATTERNS

All students of taekwondo must learn a series of **patterns** or forms, called *poomse* in Korean. Practising these patterns teaches you how to use the basic **techniques** of taekwondo. The taekwondo masters who developed the patterns made sure that they teach ways of dealing with attacks from all possible directions. The poomse also teach the proper way to carry out punches, kicks and **blocks**. They are used in **grading** exams to test students.

The moves are like training **drills** with an imaginary opponent. At first you will learn them in individual stages, as shown in the sequence on this page, but with practice you will be able to string them together smoothly. Your instructor will then teach you how to use your whole body to deliver the power of each technique to a particular place.

DIFFERENT SYSTEMS

Different taekwondo schools teach different systems of patterns. One traditional system is called *palgwe*. Many schools use a system authorized by the Korean Taekwondo Association, called *taegeuk*. The sequence shown here is made up of the first five movements of Form One in the taegeuk system, called *il-jang*.

IL-JANG

1 From the ready **stance**, turn to the left into a walking stance and perform an outer low block with the left arm.

2 Step forward one step with the right foot and punch with the right fist.

3 Pivot on your back foot as you turn clockwise to face the other way. Move your right leg to the front and perform a low block with the right arm.

4 Step forward one step with the left foot and punch with the left fist.

5 Turn to face forward again, go into a left-foot forward stance and perform an outer low block with the left arm.

The beginning of this sequence uses some of the basic techniques that we have seen earlier in the book. This first taegeuk continues with many more steps.

LEFT AND RIGHT

As in all martial arts, it is important that students can perform taekwondo techniques from both sides of the body. Every student has a favourite side, partly depending on which hand they write with, so in training they should concentrate particularly on their weaker side.

SPARRING

Sparring, or *kyorugi* in Korean, allows you to test the skills you have learned and practised with a partner. At first all the sparring is pre-arranged, which means that both opponents agree beforehand what they are going to do. This makes it easier to move on to opposed contests later. It also allows you to learn how to use combinations of attacking and defensive **techniques** properly and get your timing right.

Different taekwondo schools have varying attitudes towards sparring. Some allow only non-contact sparring, in which each strike is held back so that it does not quite reach the target. This is similar to the approach taken in **karate**. Other schools allow light contact, while some allow more vigorous contact. The amount of protective gear worn by the students depends on the type of sparring and the amount of contact.

These young students are sparring without making any contact.

These more advanced students are allowed to make light contact as they spar with each other.

COOLING DOWN

It is important to cool down gently after vigorous exercise such as taekwondo. You can do this by jogging or walking, by deep breathing and by gently stretching, as you did when you warmed up (see pages 12–13). Some students like to cool down by doing some taekwondo **pattern drills** to music.

Expert students show an advanced breaking technique.

BREAKING

Breaking techniques are used by advanced students to test and show the power of certain moves. At the opening ceremony of the 1988 Olympic Games, a taekwondo **demonstration** team used their skill to break hundreds of boards, and this is often what most people remember about taekwondo. This is obviously not something that beginners attempt, but you might see a demonstration from a taekwondo master.

GRADING

When you join a taekwondo club, you are given a licence book. Your club should also make sure you are **insured**. You use the licence book to record your progress through the taekwondo grades, all the way from beginner to expert. Levels of skill are shown by different coloured belts, which are related to a system of grades, called *kup*. You will start by wearing a white belt to show that you are at the tenth kup.

Your licence book stays with you throughout your taekwondo career.

BELT RANKS

There are five different belt colours covering the ten kup grades. When you have shown that you are on your way to the next colour, a tab on the belt shows this. So, for example, you wear a yellow tab on your white belt when you are approaching the next colour, yellow.

Kup grade		Belt colour
10th		white
9th		white with yellow tab
8th		yellow
7th		yellow with green tab
6th		green
5th		green with blue tab
4th		blue
3rd		blue with red tab
2nd		red
1st		red with black tab

At each grade there is a different set of taekwondo **techniques** to learn, and to move up to the next grade you will have to show that you can do them well. This will be tested in a **grading** exam, which may be given by your instructor. The exams vary, but you will probably have to perform basic techniques and certain **patterns**, as well as **sparring**.

It is normally expected that you have about 48 hours of training before you take each grading exam, so if you train twice a week there will be three to four months between each exam.

Taekwondo students practising for a grading exam.

BLACK BELT

The black belt is the top colour, following on from the highest kup grade. It is split up into different *dans*, or degrees. These grades are usually awarded by special judges, and the student has to train for years between each dan grade, from first dan to the very highest, ninth dan.

It usually takes about three years for a good taekwondo student to gain a black belt, but this varies according to the rules of the club and how often they train. Grades are important and are to be respected, but you will notice too that expert martial artists show complete respect for lower grades and beginners. This is an important aspect of all the **martial arts**, and you should not worry too much about which belt colour you wear. Do your best to progress at your own pace, whatever age you are when you begin.

A WORLD SPORT

Taekwondo has become an important international sport. World championships are held every two years, and taekwondo was one of just 28 sports represented at the 2000 Olympic Games. In international competition there are eight different weight divisions for both men and women, from finweight – the lightest – through to heavyweight.

Olympic and world championship taekwondo follows the rules laid down by the World Taekwondo Federation (WTF) which allow full-contact blows and kicks. Contestants must wear special headgear, a chest protector, and forearm and shin padding and groin protectors. Most competitors also wear mouthguards. The other major world organization is the International Taekwondo Federation (ITF), which allows only light contact.

RULES OF THE GAME

Taekwondo contests take place on an 8-metre square blue elastic mat, surrounded by an outer, 12-metre square. The so-called alert area outside the contest area is coloured red. Each bout is controlled by a referee, who is helped by three judges. A bout is made up of three three-minute rounds – which means that the contestants have to be super-fit!

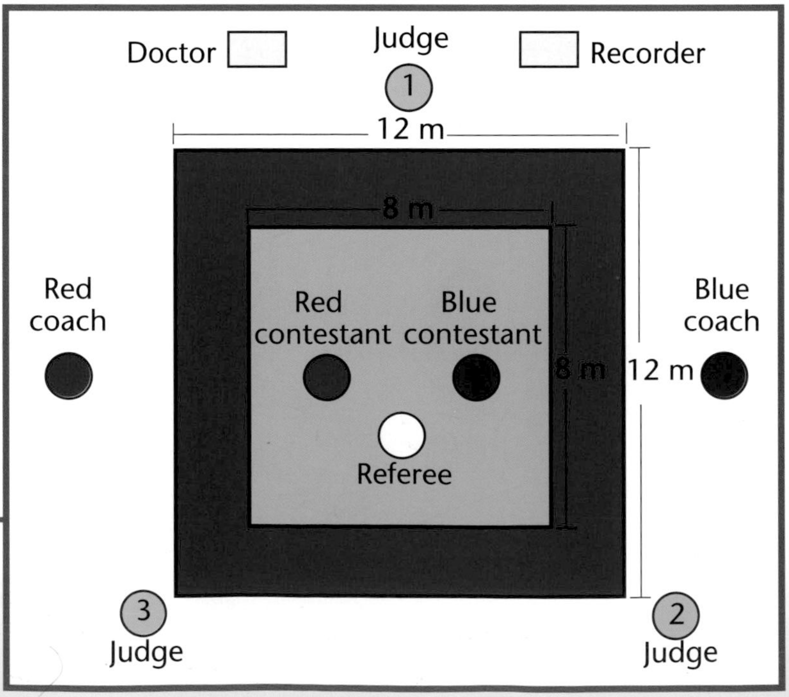

Doctor Judge 1 Recorder

12 m

8 m

Red coach

Red contestant Blue contestant

Blue coach

8 m 12 m

Referee

3 Judge

2 Judge

This diagram shows the layout of an official match area.

One of the two contestants has blue marks on his dobok and is called *chung*, and the other has red marks and is known as *hong*. Points are scored for proper blows to the target areas on the opponent. These are on the front and sides of the body above the waist for hand and foot **techniques**, and foot strikes are also allowed to the head. Points are taken away for fouls, such as grabbing, holding or pushing, and three penalty points mean immediate disqualification. If a contestant is knocked down by a proper attack, and has not recovered by the time the referee counts to ten, he or she loses the match.

If a match is a draw, the referee decides which contestant should be the winner. Any kick technique is considered better than a punch, a jumping kick is better than a standing kick and a **counter-attack** is better than an initial attack.

A total of 550 contestants from 66 different countries took part in the world championships in Edmonton, Canada, in 1999. Korea won 9 of the 16 gold medals. Prizes for the best fighting spirit went to Jordan, Brazil and Sweden.

KOREAN WORDS

You say these Korean words the way they are written here.

Korean words	Meaning	Korean words	Meaning
ap chagi	front kick	*il-jang*	the first pattern in the taegeuk series
apkoobi	forward stance		
arae makki	down or low block	*kihap*	an explosive shout that gives power
choochoom soegi	horseriding stance		
choonbi	ready or first stance	*kup*	grade
chung	blue (contestant)	*kyorugi*	sparring
dobok	taekwondo outfit	*kyungye*	bow
dojang	training hall	*momtong makki*	inner or inside block
dwi chagi	back kick	*palgwe*	a series of patterns
dwit koobi	back stance	*poomse*	patterns or forms
eolgol makki	rising or upper block	*subak*	an early form of taekwondo
hong	red (contestant)		
hwarang	flower of youth	*taegeuk*	a series of patterns
		taekkyon	an early form of Korean combat

GLOSSARY

aggressive   quarrelsome, hostile behaviour

block   an action that stops an opponent's attack

counter-attack   an attack that replies to an attack by an opponent

courtesy   polite, considerate behaviour

drill   repeating something so you learn it well

grading   marking a performance so that a student goes into a particular ability group

insured   entitled to payment if injured, after making regular payments to an insurance company

judo   Japanese martial art that uses grappling and throwing techniques

karate   Japanese martial art that uses hands and feet to make high-energy punches, strikes and kicks

kung fu   general term for all Chinese martial arts

pattern   set of moves that is learned as a training drill

spar   to have a practice contest, sometimes with the moves agreed beforehand

stance   a position of the body, with the feet in a special place and the arms held in a special way

technique   the way you learn to perform a particular skill.

BOOKS

The Ultimate Book of Martial Arts by Fay Goodman, Anness, London, 1998

The Young Martial Arts Enthusiast by David Mitchell, Dorling Kindersley, London, 1997

Top Sport: Martial Arts by Bernie Blackall, Heinemann Library, Oxford, 1998

USEFUL ADDRESSES

UK Sport
40 Bernard Street
London WC1N 1ST
020 7841 9500
www.uksport.gov.uk

Sport England
16 Upper Woburn Place
London WC1H 0QP
020 7273 1500
www.english.sports.gov.uk

Sport Scotland
Caledonia House
South Gyle
Edinburgh EH12 9DQ
0131 317 7200
www.sportscotland.org.uk

Sports Council for Wales
Sophia Gardens
Cardiff CF1 9SW
029 2030 0500
www.sports-council-wales.co.uk

Sports Council for Northern Ireland
Upper Malone Road
Belfast BT9 5LA
028 9038 1222
www.sportni.org

Martial Arts Development
  Commission
PO Box 381
Erith DA8 1TF
01322 431440
www.madec.org

National Association of Karate &
  Martial Art Schools
Rosecraig
Bullockstone Road
Herne Bay CT6 7NL
01227 370055
www.nakmas.org.uk

British Taekwondo Control Board
11 Hassocks Hedge
Northampton NN4 9QA
01604 460 800
www.btcb.org

British Taekwondo Council
163A Church Road
Redfield
Bristol BS5 9LA
0117 955 1046

World Taekwondo Federation (WTF)
635 Yuksamdong
Kangnamku
Seoul 135-080, Korea
82 2 566 2505
www.wtf.org

International Taekwondo Federation (ITF)
Drau Gasse 3
1210 Vienna, Austria
431 292 8467
www.itf-taekwondo.com

Sun Bae Taekwondo & Hapkido
159 Enoggera Tce
Paddington
Queensland 4064, Australia
617 3368 3390
www.sunbae.net

INDEX

Titles in the *Get Going! Martial Arts* series include:

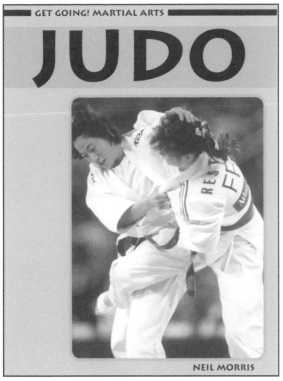

Hardback   0 431 11040 9

Hardback   0 431 11042 5

Hardback   0 431 11043 3

Hardback   0 431 11041 7

Find out about the other titles in this series on our website www.heinemann.co.uk/library